Discovering LOST DEVON

THROUGH THE MAGIC LANTERN PHOTOGRAPHS OF
THE COUNTY FROM THE TREMLETT COLLECTION

PETER THOMAS

HALSGROVE

First published in Great Britain in 2005

British Library Cataloguing-in-Publication Data
A CIP record for this title is available from the British Library

ISBN 1 84114 427 4

HALSGROVE
Halsgrove House
Lower Moor Way
Tiverton, Devon EX16 6SS
Tel: 01884 243242
Fax: 01884 243325
email: sales@halsgrove.com
website: www.halsgrove.com

Printed and bound by CPI Bath Press, Bath.

DEDICATION

In memory of
the late Murray Milton.
This book is also dedicated
to his son David

CONTENTS

INTRODUCTION – THE TREMLETT FAMILY   7

THE MAGIC OF THE LANTERN   11

EXETER   13

EXETER CATHEDRAL   45

THE EXE VALLEY   61

COCKINGTON VILLAGE   69

DEVON'S SOUTHERN COAST   75

NORTH DEVON   91

ON AND AROUND DARTMOOR   121

AROUND DEVON   141

FURTHER AFIELD – NORTH SOMERSET   151

             NORTH WALES   155

             CORNWALL   157

INTRODUCTION
THE TREMLETT FAMILY

It was nearly thirty years ago that I first became aware of this unique collection of lantern slides. I had taken a keen interest in the history of photography and was an avid collector of photographic antiques. In 1974 I was also to acquire the entire negative stock of the Henry Wykes studio in Exeter consisting of approximately 42 000 negatives. The stock contained many unique images of Exeter and was to start me on collecting photographs and images of the city in all mediums. I also did a great deal of lecturing about Exeter and photography.

I became aware of other lecturers and speakers and it was brought to my attention that a man was giving talks using magic lantern slides of old Exeter. I eventually tracked him down and discovered that he, a stockbroker in Exeter, was now living at Lydford on the edge of Dartmoor. Murray Milton and I got on extremely well and he was kind enough to allow me to copy the slides. It was later to come as a surprise when I gained a new friendship to find out that Murray was also the father of this new friend. I had the pleasure of meeting him again at his home and he told me that he used to take his lantern, a simple Johnson's Optiscope, around the local retirement homes and village halls. Many of his audience would recall details relating to the slides and often would surprise him by some of the facts they remembered. Murray had worked in Exeter for many years, was well connected and was a staunch member of Southernhay Congregational Church. He was a kind and sympathetic man and certainly appreciated the historic merit of the lantern slides.

Villa Rouge, Spicer Road, Exeter
Murray informed me that he had bought the slides at the house auction of a large property in Spicer Road, Exeter. It was called Villa Rouge (the 'Red House'), due to its façade of red sandstone dressings. The property had belonged to one of Murray's clients, Alan Tremlett, and has since become a home for the elderly called The Lodge. Murray acquired the lantern slides, being aware that they were a unique collection and a valuable local history resource.

The Tremlett Family
Murray and I talked at length about the slides and their background. He informed me that the Tremlett family, with two brothers Alan and Ernest, had a strong background in Exeter running some of the city's industries. One side of the family was involved with paper production and the other owned Tremlett's tannery, specialising in the leather and tanning trade.

I recall the tannery quite well. It could be viewed from Edmund Street, being at a lower level than the road. The road was in fact constructed on top of the remains of the medieval Exe Bridge. The higher leat ran along the back of the tannery which took water from it for the processing of leather. In Commercial Road the wide double doors would often be open showing piles of hides stacked on the floor and perhaps hanging from the ceiling. The smell was often appalling due the flensing (skinning) process.

The Tremlett Brothers
Very little is known about the background of the two brothers, Alan and Ernest, however it appears that they both had an interest in photography and that they both worked together to produce the slides. Alan Tremlett was the photographer and Ernest was involved with developing and printing, and possibly produced the actual slides. How they came to select their subjects is not known, and whether they were ever shown to the public remains a mystery.

The Slides
There is no doubt whatsoever that the images they produced, specifically on Exeter, are some of the best we shall ever see on the city at this period. The collection, of over 300, comprises views of Exeter, East Devon, South Devon, North Devon, Somerset, Cornwall and North Wales. While this book concentrates upon the Devon photographs, a few samples of other images are included in order to provide an overview of the Tremlett Collection. The quality of many images is excellent and they capture fascinating aspects of life at the time they were taken. It appears that the earliest records are those of Exeter with dates going back to 1887 and Queen Victoria's jubilee. It is likely that the latest date from the 1920s. Very few are actually dated but nearly all are captioned.

Unfortunately there is no indication as to what kind of photographic equipment was used by the brothers and how they carried out the work. There are a small number of early Dufaycolour process slides that show the interior of Villa

Rouge with its original furnishings and still life studies by Alan Tremlett. The garden is also shown with Mrs Tremlett gathering roses.

Villa Rouge Revisited

It was a natural progression to revisit Villa Rouge to see whether there was any sign of the Tremlett's lifestyle still in existence. The double-fronted villa is imposing having a central portico supported by red sandstone Corinthian columns. It resembles a small French chateau, with two lead-covered domes adding to the elegance of the building.

Today the house has lost much of its former internal character but there is still a feeling that you are walking into a significant building. Entry is through a three-arched partly-glazed door. The foyer is particularly noteworthy with an imposing mahogany staircase protected by two winged lions, each sitting on a newel post. There is a suggestion that perhaps at one time they each held a light, now missing. The decorative mosaic floor is the work of Italian artisans that were brought over from Italy specifically to carry out the task. The central feature is a rondel with floral decoration; a classical border surrounds the whole floor. The hall is partly panelled. A large wooden landing provides a good view over the mosaic floor.

A commercial lantern slide.

In the dining room the original decorative plasterwork remains but this and a few other details only hint at the genteel lifestyle of the Tremlett family. A hopeful visit to the attic failed to provide any indication that photographic processes took place there.

The Tremlett's were keen on their garden and employed a gardener. Vines were grown under glass and Mrs Tremlett was fond of roses. Today the building is a nursing home and a new extension has been constructed in the grounds.

Villa Rouge front entrance.

Looking Back

Thanks to these two brothers we are fortunate to be able to view aspects of life in the region as it was over a hundred years ago. Each original plate has been carefully examined under high magnification and printed to bring out detail that might otherwise have been overlooked. The captions accompanying each image provide further information on the individual images.

Peter Thomas
2005

The garden, Villa Rouge.

The hall.

Staircase.

Lecture Lanterns.

Nos. 21, 22 & 23, BIUNIAL.

LEVIATHAN

Illustration of **No. 23 Walnut Biunial** (ELECTRO 768).

No. 21.   Mahogany Body.   (O)

Polished mahogany body on moulded ebonised base, four panelled doors, with brass-bound sight-holes, lined metal, and fitted with dome and rose top, and side rails.   Solid brass front stages throughout, with brass curtain effect, 4 in. compound condensers, and double combination achromatic objectives, with double pinion, flashers and tinter slots, lime trays, etc. **Price, complete, £7**
Stained cabinet, with lock and key and handle, 15/-.

No. 22.   Mahogany Body.   (O)

Similar Biunial Lantern to above, with heavier body and superior finish.
Price, complete, £8 8s.
Stained cabinet, with lock and key and handle, 15/-.

No. 23.   Walnut Body (Long Focus).   (O)

Best quality **walnut body** with ornamental panelled doors and brass-bound sight-holes and flashers, lined throughout with Russian iron, fitted with heavy brass front and stages, and three-draw brass telescopic draw-tubes, compound meniscus condensers in brass cells, best double pinion cylinder jackets, with flashers and tinter slots, and fitted with double combination achromatic objectives in brass tubes, 6 in., 8 in., 10 in., or 12 in., to top and bottom. **Price, complete, £13 10s.**
Superior Cabinet, with lock and key for above, £1.
Extra cylinder tubes, each, 7/-.

A Victorian advertisement for the walnut-bodied biunial lantern slide projector.

THE MAGIC OF THE LANTERN

This book is based around a unique collection of magic lantern slides that were produced at the turn of the twentieth century. They were last seen many years ago projected in various places around Devon by the use of a Johnson's Optiscope, a simple form of lantern produced in the post-war period. Today the magic lantern has disappeared into obscurity and there are few who remember the 'magic' of a true lantern show.

The use of the magic lantern can be traced back to 1650 from which time it was to become a popular form of entertainment. Early slides were scenes painted on glass and it was the invention of the photographic process in the mid nineteenth century that saw resurgence of interest in this medium.

The instrument for projecting positive images the 'magic lantern' later became a feature in many Victorian homes but they were also used for public performances. The magic lantern is the forerunner of today's refined projector but by comparison is more like a steam engine. The use of the word 'magic' added much to the mystique of performances for many audiences who were unaware of the working of such instruments. This was often used to advantage by the lanternist

The lantern projected much larger formats than today as the use of plate cameras, using glass plates, was normal practice, and 35mm film had yet to be introduced.

The use of the magic lantern reached its peak in late Victorian times when an extensive range of apparatus was available. With mass production the most inexpensive

Magic lantern with accessories – lantern slide clamp, velvet duster and lantern slide plates.

lanterns were produced from japanned metal and fitted with a brass-mounted lens. Wooden carriers were fitted to hold the large bound glass slides. Such an instrument with its case cost one guinea around 1907.

The illuminant could be a three-wick oil lamp or, in the very cheapest models, a candle might be used. More exclusive models were produced in Russian iron with refinements, being priced at five guineas. The best models were constructed from walnut, mahogany and other fine woods, and telescopic lenses became available for use in large halls. For the true professional special instruments were available using two lenses (a biunial) or three lenses (a triunial). With these machines the professional lanternist was capable of truly spectacular shows being able to dissolve a number of slides, leaving the audience gasping at how such effects were achieved. These larger lanterns are now museum pieces.

As tehnology improved new forms of illuminants were used. These included limelight, acetylene gas, oil, paraffin, incandescent gas and electricity. However one of the most popular was carbon arc and it is still used today in some specialist circumstances. Illuminants were often dangerous and lanternists were killed due to lack of care.

The magic lantern came to be used by missionaries who showed religious slides of bible stories, religious works of art and hymns to convert 'the savage'. The effect of showing such images to the uninitiated must have created truly profound reactions. The author recalls a set of lantern slides that depicted a young native boy who preferred to visit the river instead of the church. The slides told the story of how he would be eaten by a crocodile at the river if he did not attend the church. The final images indeed showed him being swallowed by the reptile and the last slide had the young boy looking down from heaven, wishing he had joined his friends in church! Due to the availablity of simple instruments that could use almost any light source, lanterns were taken around the world to undertake 'God's work' in some of the most inhospitable places.

As has been said, the magic lantern projected images on glass that were originally hand-painted and not photographic, but with the advent of the dry glass plate use of the lantern became more popular due to mass production.

Around 1850 lantern plates were introduced with the standard size in Britain being 3.5 x 3.5 inches, and in the USA 3.5 x 4 inches. The production of slides was to become an easy process for photographers, while larger companies were to specialise in lantern slide production for the mass market. A huge range of subjects became available. Some could be purchased as sets and sometimes also had printed matter to accompany them.

Photographers were commissioned by companies and travelled the world in search of new material. Favourite subjects were architecture, buildings, works of art, views of cities, towns and villages, nursery rhymes, hymns. Comedy plays were also sold, together with an oratory. Photographers sometimes created special stage sets to record the whole sequence of a humorous play with slides being numbered and captioned. These were often given melodramatic titles such as 'Molly's Mistake'.

Initially lantern slides were in monochrome but the technique of hand-colouring became fashionable. In 1907 a hand-coloured slide cost 7 shillings and sixpence whilst the uncoloured version was 3 shillings less. Slides in the form of a coloured kaleidoscope were also popular. An artist specialising in hand colouring had to be extremely skilled, creating images that compared with nature. They were often masterpieces in their own right.

The actual production of lantern slides was a simple matter undertaken by direct contact with a glass plate. A subject would be chosen, the plate camera set up and a glass plate exposed and developed. A packet of 'blank' lantern plates could be purchased, packed in dozens, at a cost of one shilling. They were manufactured by companies such as Ilford, Paget, Wellington, Barnett, Mawson, Imperial Lumiere etc. The lantern plate would be exposed in direct contact with the exposed negative glass plate in the darkroom and then developed, becoming a positive. The emulsion side of the plate would then be protected by a glass cover. Masks could be inserted, with any hand-colouring taking place before binding with gummed Imperial binding tape.

Leviathan concentrated colours were available for colouring, with medium, palette, and brush for one shilling and sixpence. For binding purposes a clamp would be used at a cost of one shilling. A variety of screens were available made in wood or bamboo, and a typical screen for public use measured 8ft x 4ft-6 inches and came complete in a box for 35 shillings.

Very often lantern shows would be accompanied by a pianist who added music to the still images. These duties were carried out in the dark and special lamps became available to assist the pianist. They projected light without it spilling on to the screen. The 'Commodore Lamp' cost 3 shillings and sixpence.

Lanterns would often need supporting and a special stand was available. The Briton Lantern Tripod, made in polished pine, extended up to 62 inches and could be bought for 62 shillings. Slotted wooden transit boxes, holding up to 60 slides, could also be purchased to protect the images, and was ideal for the travelling lanternist. Compared with today the earlier lanternist was burdened with heavy equipment but they could be highly skilled. This element of human show-manship has now virtually disappeared, with the magic lantern rarely seen except as a museum exhibit. Although public performances are a thing of the past many lantern slides still exist and are now viewed as significant archive material. Many of the historic images captured will never be seen again. Beside the thousands of commercial slides produced it is also the work of individual private photographers that are now viewed as important local history records. If it were not for the enthusiasm of people such as the Tremlett brothers of Exeter we should not have the privilege of viewing life as it was over a hundred years ago.

Enlarging Apparatus.

THE "QUEEN" ENLARGING LANTERN. (L*)
Model B.

ELECTRO 1632.

EXETER

The eighteenth-century Exe Bridge. Exeter's three-arched stone bridge was started in 1770 and completed in 1778. In the initial stages of its construction the structure was swept away by strong floods. The problem was resolved when its foundations were placed on solid rock. Two central lamps were a feature of the bridge.

At this period the area around Exe Bridge was more intimate than today. The lantern slide shows that the water is at a low level and trees stand on the edge of the river. On the left is seen the brush factory, and on the right, immediately next to the bridge, is seen the sign of a photographic studio, at this time

occupied by H Faulkner White, whose daylight studio had a fine view over the river. The adjacent shop is occupied by D. Williams. At the end of this block is Horwill's Star and Garter public house. A motif is seen on the front façade and fine decorative railings. The bridge was demolished in 1903. No aspects shown in this photograph exist today.

The 1905 Exe Bridge. This oval lantern slide shows the replacement for the eighteenth-century Exe Bridge. The single-span steel bridge was created to allow the introduction of the electric tram. The vehicles could not be accommodated due to the arch of the previous structure. The photograph, c.1910, shows that the brush factory had been removed and that significant work had been carried out on the west bank. A new stone wall was built and the river's edge railed. It provided a new promenade and young trees have been planted. A horse and cart passes over the bridge, followed by a new electric tram on its way to St Thomas. The buildings on the Exeter side of the bridge have their shop blinds out and the corner riverside photo studio is now occupied by The Crown Photo Co. who advertise 'up to date photography'. The tall corner building seen right is Henry Turner, Furnishers, adjacent to the City Brewery.

This excellent study of Exeter Quay is taken from Haven Banks beside the ferry. A ferry service has operated across the Exe at this point since 1641. Latterly a hand wire was introduced. In the foreground are boats used for hire and at the quay's edge a wooden pair of steps leads down to give access to a number of leisure craft, one of which is being used by three men on the river, watched over by a group of children.

A fascinating aspect of this photograph is the collecting of stone by horse and cart ouside the 1835 warehouses. Another horse and cart is struggling to ascend Quay Hill after being loaded with stone. The material was possibly being used for building in the central area of the city. The original gateway to Central Warehouse Yard between the buildings is shown. The warehouse, left, bears the sign James Stokes, Wholesale. Centrally can be seen the Fountain Inn (now the Prospect Inn) next to Quay Steps and beside it Rose Cottage with its wooden fence. The property was once the home of the ferryman.

Not one of the buildings shown in the background exists today, including Central School whose bell tower is visible.

This photograph, taken at the Basin, shows a foreign vessel, *Kammerhere Schutte, Horsens* offloading. There is a cart nearby loaded with a large quantity sacks that suggest it might be coal. A branch railway line also ran nearby allowing goods to be transferred direct to railway wagons alongside the vessels. On the far side of the Basin is a large pile of sawn elm trees awaiting shipping. The stone warehouses, built in 1830, have external hoists for removing goods directly into the building.

Salmon Pool Bridge, Exeter Ship Canal. The ship canal, started in 1564, is the oldest pound lock canal in England. This section of the canal originally stood in the middle of rural countryside, linked by Clapperbrook Lane to the village of Alphington. It is shown with the older wooden swing bridge that allowed farmers to move stock. This has now been replaced with new steel version.

It was once a common sight to see horses towing vessels up the canal using the towing path. There is a suggestion of this here as horse manure litters the path. On this section of the canal a number of mature elm trees are shown, but many of these were lost in the 1960s due to Dutch elm disease. This section of the canal now links to the Marsh Barton industrial estate and is part of Exeter's Riverside Valley Park.

Edmund Street and Frog Street. There are some photographs which sum up what local history records are all about, and this is one of them. It is one of the finest archive photographs you will see from around the turn of the nineteenth century. Taken from Edmund Street, No.16 Edmund Street is shown on the corner of Frog Street. The building dates from around 1430 and is shown with a further storey. The cockloft entrance below the gable is stuffed with a rag. On the first floor, right, is a curious opening whose purpose is unknown. Although the building was rendered at a later date indications are given as to the original wooden structure by the curved frame on the first floor that oversails the street.

The ground floor, originally an open medieval shopfront, has been enclosed and glazed. In the shop window are adverts for Underwoods Malt Vinegar and Alexandra Oil. There are boxes of fruit, bottled pickles, mineral water and, stacked against the window, a large quantity of apples. A horse harness has been dropped outside.

A young girl stands in the doorway. She is suffering from rickets, having bowed legs, a common disease of the time due to nutritional deficiencies. Behind the girl, in the shop, are boxes of cabbages and sacks of potatoes. A man stands with his hands in the pockets of his cord trousers talking to a lady in a long black dress (the girl's parents?).

Frog street is shown being repaired, with a pile of stones outside a shop and two shovels resting against the wall. It is the premises of W May, Boot and Shoe Maker, who displays a poster from the Theatre Royal. Most of the road is paved with stone sets and has an open central gutter where all household waste would be emptied and washed down the street. A row of early buildings lines the street, which has a single gas lamp. On the nearer property, right, bird cages hang outside, probably containing linnets or goldfinches. Local women are fascinated by the photographer who would have been a rare sight in the West Quarter. At the end of the street a man stands with a long white apron and another stands beside a large handcart.

Tudor Street, one of Exeter's ancient back streets, is found on Exe Island adjacent to the river. The building shown is today known as the Tudor House, one of Exeter's most interesting buildings. It is shown in a reasonable state of repair at this period (c.1890) but by the mid twentieth century was dilapidated due to neglect. It was purchased by a local builder in the 1960s who painstakingly restored the property to its original state, completing the work in 1978.

It is shown here with the cellar entrance on the ground floor and above, its famous unique feature, a scalloped slate front bearing coats of arms. These possibly relate to the Gubbs family who lived in the building around 1670. It has been suggested that the building actually dates from 1630. The front façade is shown rendered which took place at a later date. On most window sills are potted geraniums. An elderly bearded man with a hat sits quietly enjoying the sun.

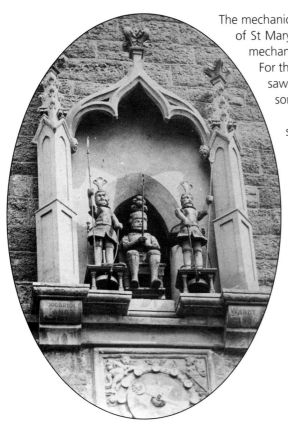

The mechanical clock 'Matthew the Miller' overlooks West Street, on the tower of St Mary Steps church. It is one of the city's more curious timepieces. A mechanical clock dating from around 1656, its true origins are obscure. For those coming to the city from the west it was the first timepiece they saw. The clock comprises three carved decorated wooden figures, some of which have been restored or replaced in recent times.

It is suggested that the central figure could be Henry VIII, supported by two javelin men. The two figures holding long hammers strike bells beneath on each quarter, and on the hour the king nods his head. Below is an astronomical clock with the four seasons, one on each corner.

For locals the clock is named after an Exeter miller who was known for his punctuality. When he died the clock was unofficially named after him and those looking up at the clock would repeat the rhyme:

Matthew the miller is alive,
Matthew the miller is dead,
But every hour on the west gate tower,
Matthew nods his head.

Houses at Stepcote Hill. Some of Exeter's oldest properties still exist in the area of the city known as the West Quarter. The fifteenth-century property shown is still one of the most important survivals of its period. The timber-framed building with the West Street sign is shown extensively rendered, hiding its earlier wooden framework. In this photograph the property is occupied by S. Cridland who advertises on the front window 'Beds'. Two young men wearing caps and boots stand in front of a large unidentified poster that is displayed next to the door. On the Stepcote Hill side, the north side, a large panelled board declares 'Stick No Bills' and the earlier fabric of the building is more visible. A feature never before seen is an iron water-hydrant with a bowl, seen at the bottom of the hill.

In the late 1920s a scheme was instigated to clear the area of slum buildings but numbers 11 and 12 West Street were saved due to the force of public opinion after a campaign to save them. Both buildings were then restored around 1930.

St Mary Steps church, West Street. The red sandstone church of St Mary Steps is of Saxon origin but was rebuilt in the fifteenth century. One of its unusual features is the steps that lead up into the church, suggesting that it is this feature that gives the building its name. To the right side of the church, on the edge of Stepcote Hill, is a small doorway and window, behind which is a tiny room. This was the original office of the porter to the west gate. It was from here that tolls were taken from those entering the city.

In front a bowler-hatted gent stands next to the water hydrant. No.11 West Street, the property of S. Cridland, displays a Theatre Royal poster advertising 'Christopher Columbus'. A lone policeman stands in the road with polished boots, strong belt and silver buttons, projecting an air of authority. His appearance is completed with a thick handlebar moustache.

Police would often walk in twos as the West Quarter area was notorious. The single lampost was a feature and the church railings were removed for the war effort in the Second World War. A small shop to the left of the church, named Tuckers, advertises Champions Mustard, and piles of apples are displayed in the window.

The Coronation procession of 1902 was perfectly captured by Alan Tremlett from the spot known as Horsepool in Edmund Street adjacent to Tremlett's tannery. The event was a grand historical pageant consisting of sixteen tableaux representing the history of Exeter from earliest times. The pageant route started and ended at the Higher Barracks after processing through much of the city. It was followed by the mayor's dinner for the elderly that took place in Northernhay. Hundreds of people lined the streets, taking advantage of any high vantage point.

Three front riders appear to be dressed as early courtiers with the main tableaux filled with people in Elizabethan costume. The painted background, a church interior, has men following with royal banners. At the front right, a bowler-hatted gent smokes a pipe looking rather pensive about the whole thing. Two children (centre) hold hands, the older boy perhaps explaining the pageant to his younger brother. A billboard in the background proclaims the new tourist season for the Great Western Railway; it is dated 1902.

The main attraction is a fire appliance of 1616 and aboard are five men dressed in early uniforms. The appliance was one of a pair, the other being kept at Windsor Castle. The Exeter engine was often displayed in carnivals and events and was lastly used in the great Theatre Royal fire of 1887. In front a man rides a horse dressed as city trumpeter. To the rear a royal personage wearing an ermine cape is escorted by soldiers and other noted gentlemen of the seventeenth century.

The pageant is now just passing St Edmunds church and it is here that the viking period is portrayed brandishing shields and wearing winged helmets. The procession is viewed from upstairs windows by women and children. Groups of ladies wearing large hats decorated with flowers enjoy every moment. The central building advertises 'Suits to Measure, 30 shillings, Cornish and Co for Gents and Boys Outfitting. The Best Value, Cornish and Co. Outfitters and Tailors'. The property may have been a supplementary warehouse. Cornish's supplied all types of general clothing.

New Bridge Street, a viaduct, was constructed to link up with the new Exe Bridge and was completed in 1778. It provided easier access to the river, although the steepness of Fore Street could still cause problems for horses and, after 1905, electric trams. Horse-drawn traffic is shown in this record of about 1890. It was popular to advertise by using posters and numerous are shown, including one for Yorkshire Relish.

Joshua Daw has a large window display featuring 'Easy fitting hats at Scotland House', while at 32 New Bridge Street C E Cann advertises 'the people's watchmaker, repairs in all branches, best for house plate.' A poster also advertises E A Marriott of 235 High Street, to promote their pianos. At this point two people look over at the higher leat that flows beneath the street while two men pass by in a pony and trap. From a parked carriage a man talks with the driver of a pony and trap. Numerous shops have their blinds out. These were supported by brass poles inserted into the edge of the kerb.

Preston Street and Rack Street. At this period it was very rare for a photographer to be seen in back streets. This excellent record of around 1896 shows Preston Street which is one of the smaller streets leading down to the river from behind South Street. It clearly shows some of Exeter's finest medieval timber-framed buildings in excellent condition. These important period buildings were torn down in the 1930s. The eminent architect James Crocker extolled the virtues of these buildings in 1895.

The narrow entrance to the left led to Rack Street and the Victorian Central School. This catered for many of the children of the West Quarter. The Rack Street sign is clearly shown. The street is shown laid out with stone sets and a central gutter, a common layout in earlier times. Waste would be thrown out of the window into the central gutter.

In the shop window (left) there is an advert for Venus Soap, Camp Coffee, Watson's Matchless Cleanser, along with biscuits, and jars containing rock. A glass-covered box holds small household items (buttons etc). From the top window of the house next door a woman peers down to see what is going on.

This view looks down Fore Street from the junction with South Street. Traditionally the Fore Street was home to many trades throughout the centuries.

To the far left is shown H C Lloyd's cigarette factory. The company had a history stretching back to 1784. Their products included all types of cigarettes, cigars, tobacco, and snuff. The company was to close in the early twentieth century due to free tobacco being sent to the troops during the 1914–18 war. Lloyds promoted themselves by producing cigarette cards bearing photos of fashionable people and pretty ladies for which their female staff were often persuaded to be models. Lloyd's cigarette cards are now eargerly sought by collectors.

No.78 Fore Street was owned by C Ham, and his advert is seen on the wall. He sold wine, spirits, ale, cider, stout, whisky and mineral waters amongst other products. No.79, next door is shown as Decorative House, a paper-hanging warehouse. Past this property a man pulls a handcart, accompanied by a boy with a large wicker basket over his back. In front of them is the West of England Boot and Shoe Company and the upstairs is a restaurant and reading room. C Oliver, also boot sellers are next door, identfied by three large external lamps. An array of boots are on display.

This photograph shows two of Exeter's finest historic buildings. Standing at the top of Fore Street, Nos.78 and 79 had been integrated after 1940 to create the Chevalier Inn. The title did not come about by accident as an equestrian statue stood on the gable of No.79. However in this photograph of 1895 the statue has been removed. Such ridge tiles were recorded in the South West from 1600 but that custom died out by 1700. There appears to be no known reason for their existence. Such tiles were apparently made at the brickworks at Bridgetown, Totnes

In 1879 the architect James Crocker sketched the buildings and included them in his book *Old Exeter*. He states 'This is by far the best example of seventeenth century work in Fore Street, one of the houses being occupied by Mr Jerred, a wine merchant, and the other by Mr Sanders, a chemist. There was considerable interference with the exterior of the buildings but both had been faithfully preserved with all woodwork being of true British oak. The interiors contained decorative plaster work.'

At the time shown No.78 is occupied by Charles Ham wine and spirit merchant. The original business had been established in 1829 and was one of the oldest in the city. On the front of No.79 is a Fire Assurance plaque. A horse and cart stands in the street laden with bamboo poles, flower pots, a number of packages tied with string, and a wicker basket. A boy sits on the cart with his hand over his mouth, while a newspaper boy stands outside No.79. A bowler-hatted man chats with a fishmonger under the type of tassled canopy that was once a familiar sight in Exeter.

This early rare image of North Street emphasises the quality of buildings that once graced this area of the city. In partic-ular the group on the end of the street near the Iron Bridge was of particular interest, with a double-fronted building dating from the late sixteenth century. It was noted for its fine windows, carvings and rare lead gutter. It is shown here intact but was to be demolished in 1890, shortly after this photograph was taken. Only the windows were retained and deposited in the City Council yard where they remained until 1930, finally being inserted into a reconstructed building adjacent to Gandy Street in the High Street in 1930.

In this view a sign is shown to the left, beside a passageway that led to the rear. It states 'Hancock, Ticket, Sign & Showcard Writer'.

Children gaze intrigued by the photographer, whilst women gossip in the street. An empty shop window advertises 'To Let'. No.17 shown under the name of Spiller advertises 'tea, coffee, beds and rooms'. In the adjacent butcher's shop chickens and rabbits are hung up and meat is laid out on slabs.

On the corner of the No.20 North Street a horse and cart stands with the sign John Lock, Baker and Confectioner, of 66 St Sidwells, 96 Queen Street and 23 Goldsmith Street. There was a small square on this section of North Street. A sign on the wall states W & A Hellier, Family Butchers, and underneath, Wilson and Sons, Timber Merchants and Yard.

In the distance people walk up St David's Hill and horse and carts are making their way out of Exeter. The small iron-work bridge connecting the Barnstaple Inn with the Iron Bridge can also be seen.

For Queen Victoria's Jubilee in 1897 Mr Tremlett recorded the recreated south and north city gates. The North Gate is shown here at the beginning of the Iron Bridge on the city side. The structure was created from wood and plaster, then painted.

A young man holds a wheelbarrow and next to him another wears a large white apron. A group of people, including a lady with a handcart, have gathered to be photographed in front of the new attraction. The corner premises, left, displays an advert for 'John Guest, the Reliable Firm, Est. 1848, 199 High Street, Exeter. Pianos, organs, harmoniums, lower prices, highest value.'

Stephens' shop is decorated with laurel, and a poster for Fry's Cocoa is displayed. Outside a man is dressed in a railway uniform.

The Iron Bridge is garlanded with evergreens and two carts are leaving the city. To the right a business called Glades was later the become the *Express & Echo* sports club.

Paul Street today has been totally lost to unsympathetic development. Detailed records of it are scarce. This particular photograph is one of the very few that gives any indication as to what the old street really looked like. The narrow street that backed on to the city wall, led to the north gate and comprised many small dwellings and businesses. The photo is c.1894.

Towards the end of the nineteenth century and the early part of the twentieth century the area was gradually cleared. According to a street directory of 1894, when the street was last intact, Paul Street contained the Anchor Inn, a greengrocer, hairdresser, bootmaker, butcher, St Paul's Sunday school, a general store, painter, marine stores, a leather seller, fruiterer, a wood and coal dealer, and an ale and porter stores. All of these, including private dwellings, were removed by 1924 with the exception of the Sunday school.

Paul Street contained a number of courts and alleyways with interesting names: Hearn's Court, Cornish's Court, Barbican Place, Victoria Place, Richmond Place, St Paul's Place, Maddock's Row and Anthony Buildings. Before the Second World War the north side of the street was utilised as a coach and bus station.

Alan Tremlett was to record the ancient gateway of Rougemont Castle. The original Norman gate is seen left with the later addition, with the portcullis on the right

In 1891 human bones were found just inside the gate creating a great deal of curiosity. Reports on the history of the castle appeared at the time in the papers stating 'there is no authenticated record as to the age of the fortifications known as Rougemont and that only conjecture can relate to specific dates of its construction'. The extensive article commented further opinion on its origins but also stated 'only one of these gateways now remain namely, the ivy covered ruin on the left side on the main entrance from castle street. The relic affords ample evidence of the great strength of the castle'.

In 1770 several houses were taken down in Castle Street to widen the throughfare. The old gateway was demolished and in levelling the road (which may be seen by inspecting the side of the aforementioned ruin abutting Castle Street), which is some four or five feet lower than formerly, the foundation of the ancient drawbridge which crossed the fosse was discovered. The present gateway was built with the materials from these foundations, a sham portcullis being added. The insertion of a gas lamp would appear strange indeed to medieval eyes.

Forty years later a guide book described the new gateway somewhat acidly: 'The ancient gateway has been restored, the ivy torn from its walls, old stones

replaced by new, and every crack and corner industriously filled with cement. The result is that this relic is as smart and spick and span as any ruin in England and no one who views it can forget it is a restoration.'

In 1863 a statue was erected to Earl Fortescue, Lord Lieutenant of Devon as a memorial, in the courtyard of Rougemont Castle. It faced the visitor as they entered the site. The inscription on the base read 'This memorial marking the love of friends and the respect of all was erected in 1863.'

The year of this photo is 1896, as stated on a poster displayed on the billboard to the left of the shop front. Also advertised are train journeys to the Empire and India and Ceylon Exhibition, Madame Tussauds, the Grocers Exhibition and the Crystal Palace. Fares range from ten to seventeen shillings.

The building, dating from approximately 1600, had a long history as a butcher's shop on the ground floor. It was however originally a three-storeyed dwelling of timber-frame construction with two Heavitree stone chimney stacks. Latterly the ground floor had been gutted to create a shop. This photograph is a classic record of one of the city's early butcher shops showing an open front with meat and poultry hanging on hooks in the open air – a common practice. The butcher is seen peering out from between the meat. To the right is hanging a fore of lamb, whole lamb and a breast and a quarter of beef, and to the right a loin of lamb. Legs and shoulders of lamb hang from the rails. A large cleaver is lying in the window. The property is trading under the name Maddicks. It appears the ground floor is divided with a doorway and another closed window. The adjacent shop belongs to Palmer and Co. Ices are advertised in the window, while a large glass display dishes stand empty.

In the south tower of Exeter cathedral hangs one of the heaviest peals of bells in the world. The huge tenor bell is called the Grandisson Bell, named after the bishop from whom it was a gift. The bell weighs 72cwt. A heavier bell, Great Peter, hangs in the north tower and weighs 125cwt. In 1901 the Dean and Chapter became worried about the state of the bells and it was decided to check them. It was found that rehanging was imperative as constant strain and wear on the timbers had started to affect the ringing. It was decided to reconstruct the bell cage and this was carried out using steel rather than wooden bearers. The strain of ringing would be minimised and the easy swing would be marked by a more regular and musical striking.

To mark the coronation of King Edward VII it was decided to have the bells ready to mark the occasion. The Grandisson Bell was to be recast and sent to Messrs Taylor of Loughborough who were to carry out the work. After recasting, the bell was removed by crane from the train. The date 1729 is clearly seen on the top of the bell. It was carried to the cathedral by horse and cart.

The Dean and Chapter instigated the recasting of the tenor and fifth bells from the cathedral at a cost of £1700. The Dean paid for the recasting of the fifth bell and the rest was paid by public subscription. By 24 June 1902 the bells were free from debt and the dedication service took place. A motto on the fifth bell reads in Latin:

'Called from the pit, we scale the starry heights, arise!
And follow in our upward flight.'

Due to the ingenious new gearing the bells could now be rung by one man. The Grandisson Bell is shown on its arrival at the west front of the cathedral on a horse and cart. The horse has been taken out of its shafts. Two men, one holding a rolled umbrella, admire the bell while a child taps it to see if it rings! To the far left a woman appears to be heavily pregnant and holds her hands across her middle. To the far right a child wears a sailor suit, fashionable at the time. He has one sock up and the other down.

In Exeter's Cathedral Close remains a charming group of buildings known as the Quadrangle. It is entered by a fine studded wooden door of c.1600. The group of buildings, used for ecclesiastical purposes, comprises what was once a refectory, buttery, kitchen, offices, hall and chapel that form the sides of a courtyard. Parts of these buildings can be traced back to the fourteenth century. Despite changes throughout the centuries this complex still retains its old-world charm. The courtyard still has an ancient hand-pump with a large stone trough, and a tudor doorway over which are the arms of Bishop Oldham who lived in the reign of Henry VIII. The court-yard is particularly well known for its magnificent wysteria.

One of Exeter's finest architectural treasures is the door to No10 The Close. It is one of a few rare early doors in Exeter dating from c.1600. The massive studded oak door is beautifully carved and features a smaller central wicket door that allowed only pedestrians to enter the courtyard. The whole door could be opened to allow a horse and carriage to enter.

Around 1895 Alan Tremlett recorded one of the city's finest buildings, Mol's Coffee House in the Cathedral Close. At this time it was occupied by Messrs Worth & Co., an art gallery, framers and picture restorers. The company produced a great number of historical images of Exeter for retail sale and promoted local artists. Worth's were particularly noted for their postcards and Mr Worth took a special interest in his building and published his findings in a city guide. He concluded that it had once been used as a club under royal authority up until 1806. Hence the royal coat of arms on the front of the building. The original was later removed and a painted replica made. On the first floor of this sixteenth-century building is the panelled oak room displaying forty-six coats of arms relating to famous Devon families including Drake and Raleigh. The name, 'Mol' is a reference to an early Italian owner.

Worth & Co. promoted the history of their building with a large decorative board stating: '1596 Elizabethan oak panelled room, the meeting place of our naval and military generals who fought the Spanish Armada. Open free to visitors daily.' Above this board is written: 'Formerly Mol's Coffee House'. The decorative gable and balcony were much later additions to the building.

The Norman gateway to the castle is shown covered with ivy. It was to be later restored. Beyond it, within the castle courtyard stood the original porter's lodge. In 1891 the building's sanitary arrangements were inspected and it was found that the front room floor was decaying. On pulling up the floorboards a human skull was found along with a number of other small bones. On examination it was thought they had lain there for many years, possibly since before the sixteenth century. In the dead of night on 23 June 1891 two workmen carried a coffin out of the castle to the cemetery.

Situated in the very heart of Exeter and adjacent to Rougemont Castle these delightful gardens were opened to the public in 1912. Previously they had been privately owned. The gardens were created around the moat of the castle in the late 1800s by Exeter surgeon, John Patch. The photo shows a gardener who is at work on the slope leading up to the castle. He has hung his coat over a sapling.

Rougemont Castle was constructed in the northern corner of the original city at its highest point. At its north aspect the castle wall is at its highest and overlooks Northernhay, now the oldest public park in the country.

Mrs Tremlett is seen resting on a bench at St John's Tower that overlooks the park giving exceptional views to the north. The tower was a later decorative addition, not intended for defence.

Northernhay Gardens, the oldest public gardens in England were laid out in 1612 and described as 'a pleasant walk on Northernhay'. It has continued to be an oasis in the centre of the city for centuries. The park has been embellished with a number of statues of historical personalities, adding to the elegance of the site.

On entering the park at the east gate, off Northernhay Place, the bronze statue of the deerstalker is seen. It stands on a large granite pedestal and is the work of E B Stephens ARA. The work was presented to the city by a number of his friends and admirers in 1878 and depicts an athletic Scot with a deerhound waiting to pursue its prey. The statue originally stood in Bedford Circus but was later moved to the gardens.

The statue of the Earl of Iddesleigh, which is carved in marble, was the work of the sculptor Boehm. It was unveiled by Lord Clinton on 19 October 1887.

The statue to Thomas Dyke Acland was unveiled on 22 October 1861. The work of the sculptor E B Stephens it is made of marble and stands on a polished granite plinth. It was erected 'as a tribute to mark his public integrity, generous heart and open hand without regard to party, race or creed, and his willingness to protect the weak, relieve the needy and succour the oppressed'. He was an MP for many years from 1812 until 1857, being re-elected several times.

This elegant plinth in grey granite and Portland stone is a memorial to Sir John Bucknill the promoter of the First Rifle Volunteers. Part of the design is a medallion bust with inscriptions. The plinth was the work of Exeter ecclesiastical carver Harry Hems and was erected in 1895.

This photograph, taken at 9.34am according to the clock, is of the Miles Memorial Clock Tower and shows Elm Grove Terrace in the background. The tower, erected by Mrs Miles of Dixs Field, was a memorial to her husband, a local philanthropist and lover of animals. Built in Chudleigh limestone and red Corsehill it served both as a timepiece and as a watertrough for horses. Each corner was decorated with electric lamps. On the east side is a fountain for weary travellers. At night the clock dial was illuminated internally.

Photographic records not only capture historic views but also reflect on the tastes of society at the time they were taken. In this case the subject is architecture. This rare photographic image of the original early nineteenth century St David's church was taken in 1896 at 12.48pm. It was nicknamed the 'pepper pot church' because of its style. Its foundation stone was laid on 4 June 1816 to mark the birthday of George III. This graceful building was demolished in 1897.

Before the Second World War the city of Exeter boasted some of England's finest buildings, many of them being found in High Street. Two noted example were Nos.226 and 227 dating from the sixteenth and seventeenth centuries. In this fine lantern slide the sixteenth-century 226 High Street is occupied by A Mashford, Milliner and Ladies Hatter, and the printing offices of the *Devon Evening Express* and *Devon Weekly Times*. W Symons, watchmaker and jeweller also conducted his business from here. An elaborate lamp hangs on the front of building. Some twenty years later this property was to be restored.

No.227 High Street is, at this time, occupied by J G Ross tailors and outfitters, also dealers in hats and umbrellas. The company also specialised in riding gear of the highest quality. The High Sherriff of Devon utilised the company for heralds' uniforms, banners and other regalia. J G Ross was also one of the largest shirt makers in the South West. The public house, the Civet Cat, is seen next door, and a figure is also seen in a doorway bearing a yoke carrying pails of milk.

This delightful fountain originally stood at the top of Southernhay Gardens almost opposite the Congregational Church. It is the only known record of this fountain and as yet no information about it has been found. It is shown covered in ice after a severe snowfall. There is a possiblility that this could be as early as 1891 when the Great Blizzard swept through Devon causing major devastation. Nor is it known when this graceful feature disappeared from its site.

This excellent photograph shows Catherine Street running from the Cathedral Close to Bedford Street. It displays all the delights of Exeter's ancient back streets, being lined with period timber-framed buildings on an intimate scale. Today the character of this street is virtually lost. Before the Second World War the street extended twice as far into the central area.

In 1895 twenty-nine trades operated from the street. To the left is seen the window of William Roberts, the tailor, adjacent to the London and West of England Yeast Co who advertise desiccated coconut, blanched almonds, and ground almonds. The proprietor is having discussions with two young boys.

In No.3 Catherine Street, Willey & Son, gasfitters, plumbers and sanitary engineers operate. A sign states: 'Pneumatic bells fixed and repaired here'. At No.4 is Gibbons & Co fishmongers. Theirs is an open-fronted shop with fish displayed on slabs and hung on hooks. A small canopy shades the shopfront. The property next door is the Swan Inn, at this time run by Ann Foster.

This classic scene of Nos.41 and 42 High Street is one of the finest records of the city's buildings. Originallly two gabled timber-frame buildings, as shown here, the properties were to be later joined together. A carved doorhead bore the date 1564. No.41 is shown here occupied by Hinton Lake chemists and photographic retailers. They supplied Exeter with some of the earliest box cameras and developing equipment, and later sold pocket Kodaks and Ilford panchromatic plates. In the street stands a horse and cart with four milk churns and hand jugs, used for delivering milk. A woman and five children are fascinated by the photographer.

No.42 is operating as the Gospel Depot and Publishing Office. Outside the depot stand two young boys and a child dressed in a sailor suit. At No.43 is John Elliott Lake, jewellers. The front of the building is boarded. These fine buildings had long been recognised as being of historical and architectual significance and appear in the nineteenth-century book, *Old Exeter,* by architect James Crocker. Today they are the premises of Laura Ashley.

To celebrate Queen Victoria's Jubilee the city decided to erect copies of the old city gates. Photographic records of the south gate and north gate only are known to exist, both taken by Alan Tremlett in 1897. The south gate, created in plaster and wood, was erected immediately outside the White Hart hotel in South Street. The gate was painted and topped by three flags. A man has stopped his horse and cart to have a chat. The street is shown in its original width which continued to the junction with Magdalen Street, half its present-day width. On the right is the entry to Coombe Street where hangs a decorative sign advertising 'Gibbs & Company Tea Merchants'

This is thought to be the earliest known photographic image of Trews Weir Mill. It stands beside the River Exe at Trews Weir. The origins of the building are obscure but it is recorded as being a flax mill in the mid nineteenth century when a retting pond for soaking flax existed beside the mill. The property was to become known as the Old Match Factory after the erection of a metal sign by the then owner Mr Pitts. The sign had, it is said, come from a building in the area of Sidwell Street and had no connection with the mill or the industry carried out there.

The Seven Stars Hotel stood on the corner of Okehampton Street and Exe Bridge. Adjacent to it was Randalls, a seed merchant whose window is seen right. Numerous trophies are in the window. The Seven Stars Hotel had an extensive rear riverside balcony from where boats could be hired. The hotel had a long association with theatre in Exeter and a large internal staircase was sometimes used for impromptu theatrical performances.

In the street a man wearing a peaked cap looks at the notice board advertising a 'Horitz Passion Play'. At this time the hotel was called Howards Seven Stars Hotel and a large external signboard states 'Well aired beds, good stabling, pleasure boats for hire, good skittle alley'.

A corner of the riverside village of Countess Wear is shown, with a small girl standing in a doorway. The village, at this time outside the city, contained a number of typical thatched Devon cottages and was very rural. The roads are seen as rough tracks. The construction of a stone lime kiln on the river's edge allowed the offloading of the raw material used for fertiliser. It was brought upriver by shallow-draughted barges. The remains of the kilns still exist today.

Cowley is a hamlet of Upton Pyne and is noted for its fine bridge. The lantern slide shows the view upriver where, in the distance, the Queen Anne house, Pynes, is seen. The view shows the railway bridge that carries the Crediton line during winter, with copius amounts of water coming down the River Exe.

Sunset over Exeter.

EXETER CATHEDRAL

The view of Exeter Cathedral from the Bishop's Palace garden is unsurpassed. The palace is shown covered with virginia creeper on its upper parts and the lower with ivy. At ground level the three open archways, now infilled, once connected with the now demolished extensive western range. This section, now the lawn, was truncated during the sixteenth and eighteenth centuries.

The famous west front of Exeter Cathedral is shown blackened by age and pollution. The façade has some of the finest medieval statuary in the country. For centuries a road had existed in front of the building. The corner of St Mary Major church is seen right. Elm trees were once a common sight in the cathedral yard.

The northern prospect is shown with the north tower. It appears the Cathedral Close has been recently laid out with fresh turf and crossed with a series of defined paths. Each section has been wired off. A single tree remains.

The south tower of the cathedral is seen from the grounds of the Bishop's Palace. Oldham's tower, with its oriel window, takes its name from Bishop Oldham. This original fourteenth century entry to the palace was extended in the nineteenth century with the addition of an embattled top storey. The large stone bow window left, known as the Elyot window is an addition inserted into the building in the nineteenth century. It was removed from a building in the Cathedral Yard adjacent to St Petrock's church.

The south side of the Bishop's Palace showing the Elyot window.

East view of the cathedral from the Bishop's Palace. The full extent of the roof, 300 feet long, can be seen together with the towers and lady chapel.

The Nave and the spectacular decorated gothic roof of the cathedral is shown looking towards the John Loosemoore organ built in 1665.

Opposite: The Quire and organ. This unusual view was taken from the Clerestory, a walkway that extends around the interior below roof level. The early fourteenth century bishop's throne is seen left and beyond are the choir stalls dating from the eighteenth century. Rare thirteenth-century carved seats, misericords, can still be seen in the stalls.

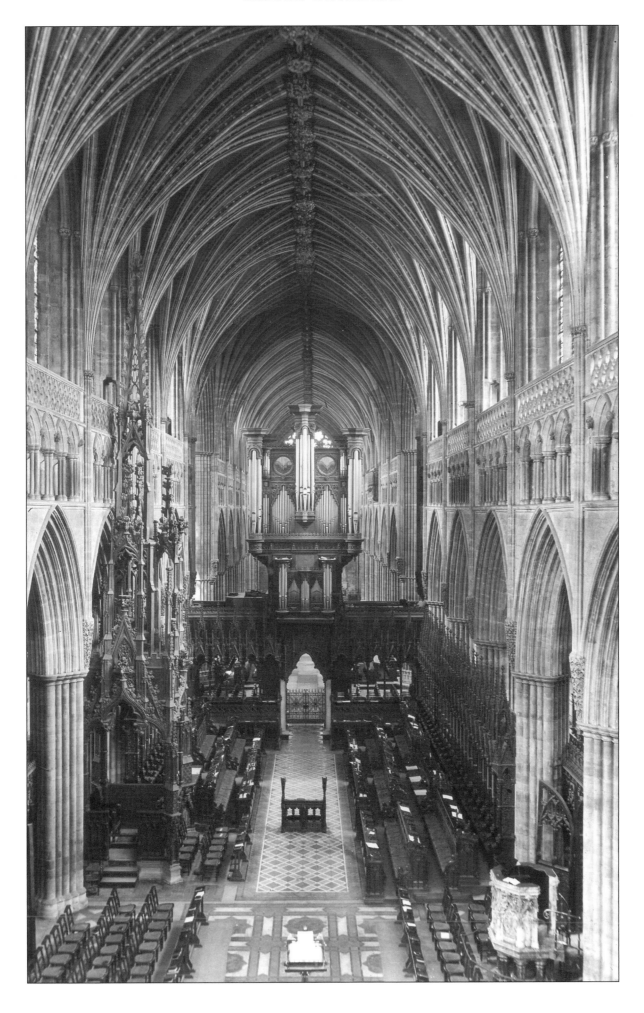

The John Loosemoore organ. The cathedral archives show that an organ was used as early as 1280. In 1665 John Loosemoore built the huge organ that dominates the nave. Its massive bass pipes stand in the south transept. The organ was rebuilt in 1876 and enlarged in 1891. In 1933 further work was carried out and, although damaged in 1942, the instrument was reassembled and again overhauled in 1965.

The effigies of Hugh Courtenay, Earl of Devon, and his wife Magaret Bohun lie in the south transept. The figures date from the 1400s and rest on what was a fourteenth-century tomb chest.

This view looks down on the south transept and clearly shows the Courtenay tomb. These figures were removed from the Courtenay chantry that at one time stood in the south arcade of the nave. The huge organ pipes are seen left.

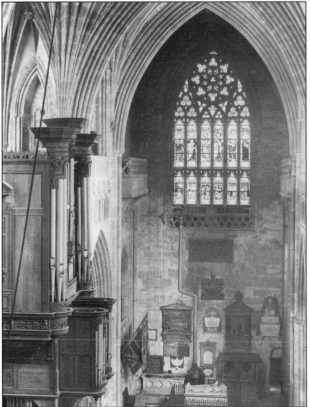

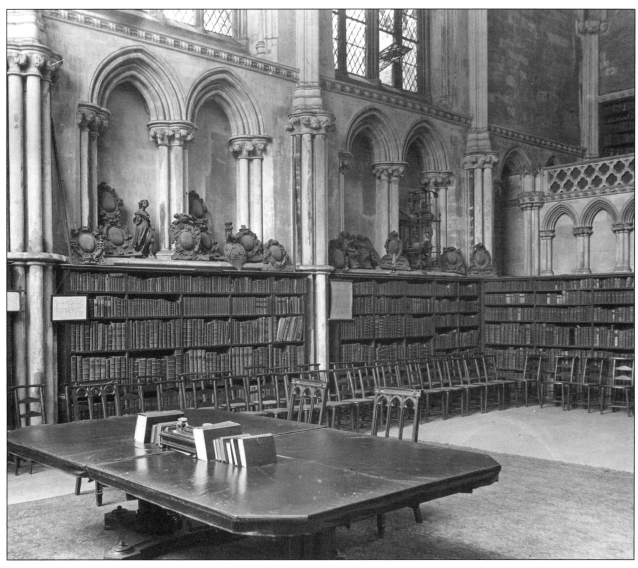

In the thirteenth century Bishop Brewer built a Chapter House on a site that was originally part of the Bishop's Palace garden next to the cathedral. The building was used for the cathedral library for a time, with books lining the walls. The library today is in the Bishop's Palace. Various unused decorative wall plaques are seen propped up in the niches.

The Chapter House library.

Opposite: The focal point in the north transept is the late fifteenth-century clock given by Bishop Peter Courtenay. It was restored in the eighteenth century. The astronomical clock features a central globe that revolves around the moon.

This rare image shows St James' Chapel on the south side of the cathedral near the tower. It was totally destroyed during the Exeter blitz in May 1942.

This fine decorated tomb is the focal point of the Oldham Chantry, dedicated to Bishop Oldham who died in 1519. A feature of his coat of arms is the figure of an owl.

The figures of Sir John Doddridge and his wife are to be found in the Lady Chapel. Sir John, a judge, is dressed with a black cap and ruff and was originally a free-standing statue. Lady Doddridge is reclining and wearing clothes which were the height of fashion in her time.

This fine wall monument is dedicated to Dr Edward Cotton the Cathedral Treasurer who died in 1675. The bust is of a particularly fine quality.

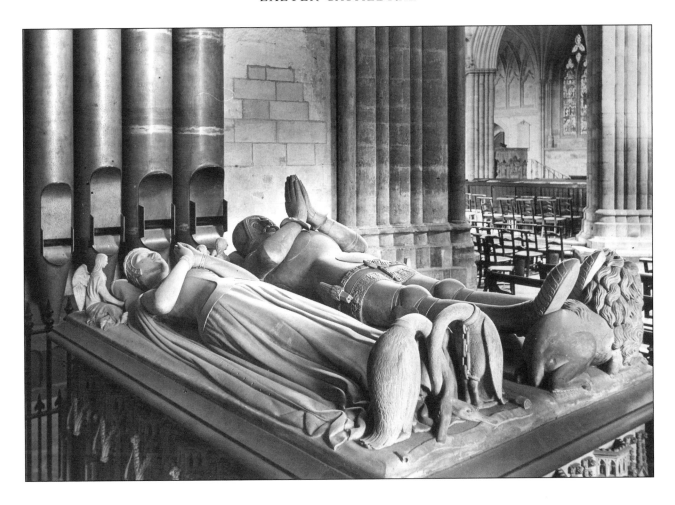

The tomb of the Earl and Countess of Devon. Hugh Courtenay, dressed in armour, has his feet on a resting lion whilst his wife has swans entwined at her feet, part of her family coat of arms.

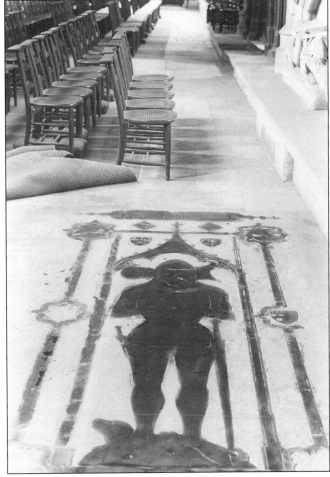

An armorial brass uncovered in the south transept.

A misericord bearing a rare thirteenth-century carving of an elephant

Misericord – a royal figure.

Misericord – cock and dragon.

Misericord – the green man.

THE EXE VALLEY

The road through the Exe Valley approaching Stoke Canon. The bridge can be traced back to the thirteenth century but a new structure was built in the late eighteenth century and flood arches constructed in the early nineteenth century. The bridge is over 800 feet long.

Built in 1835 St Mary Magdalene Church at Stoke Canon is shown with ivy covering its tower. According to the clock the photo was taken at 2.15pm.

The five-arched stone bridge over the River Exe at Bickleigh.

The New Inn at Bickleigh is shown as one of a number of small cottages. The cottage, right, has a postbox in the wall. Partly covered in ivy the cottage verandah has a new corrugated iron roof. At this point the river is approached by a gentle slope.

A later photograph of Bickleigh shows the riverbank has been reinforced and the cottage has changed appearance.

A delightful record of the post office at Bickleigh. A post box is seen in the wall and above the top window are protruding figures 170 RPE. At the cottage, right, a lady stands in the door with bird cages on each side of her.

Bickleigh church tower has origins dating back to the thirteenth century but the building was substantially rebuilt in the mid nineteenth century.

The interior of Bickleigh church.

Bickleigh Castle stands on an idyllic site in the Exe Valley. The sandstone gatehouse, although altered and repointed, is an important feature. A fine Italian wrought iron gate is an elegant later addition.

Shobrooke House, near Crediton, was destroyed by fire and the remains pulled down in 1947. The building had been remodelled in the mid nineteenth century in an Italianate style. The fine gardens still remain. The park is shown with a herd of fallow deer.

COCKINGTON VILLAGE

The small village of Cockington in Torbay lies in a valley adjacent to Cockington Court. Its location and charming pictur-esque cottages has made it a tourist attraction for over a century. In the 1930s a trust was formed to retain the village and preserve its character. The old village forge was to become a focal point for visitors.

The forge c.1890.

The original farmhouse in the centre of Cockington.

A young lady stands in the doorway of rustic cottage in the village.

A thatched lodge was constructed in 1838 at the entrance to the grounds of Cockington Court. The cottage was designed with a verandah created with rustic tree limbs.

St George and St Mary is a typical Devon church, possibly dating from the fifteenth century but restored in the late nineteenth century.

Cockington Court was originally the seat of the Cary family from the fourteenth century to the mid seventeenth century but later became the property of Roger Mallock, an Exeter merchant. The estate remained with the Mallock family until the 1930s. The original Tudor building was altered in the seventeenth century and again in the nineteenth century. Mrs Tremlett and a friend are seen walking in the grounds in the early 1930s.

DEVON'S SOUTHERN COAST

The River Dart at Dartmouth, South Devon. This view from Dartmouth to Kingswear shows a large sailing vessel moored at Kingswear. The stern of a steam boat is shown right, at the quay.

The naval training vessels *Britannia* and *Hindostan* are seen moored in the Dart estuary. The ships are connected by a covered communicating tunnel. The vessels were replaced by Dartmouth Royal Naval College in 1905. The vessels were removed from the estuary in 1910.

The River Dart is seen as a haven for smaller vessels.

A detailed record of the naval training vessels, *Britannia* and *Hindostan* c.1900.

The Butterwalk, Duke Street, Dartmouth, South Devon. Dartmouth's famous Butterwalk, dating from the mid 1600s, is seen from the quay and occupied by, among others, Scammel, Boot and Shoe Maker. A sign, seen right, exhorts visitors to see 'the old room where King Charles held his court-with the original mantelpiece'. A tobacconist and hairdresser operate from the end of the Butterwalk. A handcart has been left in the street.

The Butterwalk c.1890 looking down Duke Street.

Brixham Quay, South Devon, looking towards Fore Street. The quay is revealed here as a working port with the Fishermen's Institute shown centre, and right, Collings the Ironmonger. Two horse-drawn covered wagons stand on the quayside.

Brixham Quay c.1930.

The statue of William of Orange, Brixham, commemorating the landing of the Prince in 1688.

Brixham Quay with the Sea Cadet band. Two large cannon stand on each side of the statue of William of Orange while ladies pushing perambulators chat on the quayside.

A sunken vessel lies in Torquay harbour, South Devon. The view looks towards Holy Trinity church, with Vaughan Parade, seen left.

Teignmouth, South Devon. The harbour is shown with many sailing vessels. In earlier times the port sent vessels to Newfoundland for cod.

Teignmouth harbour – a fisherman repairs his boat.

An unusual record of a moonlight night on the Teign estuary.

Sailing on the River Teign. It is possible that the person seen here is one of the Tremlett brothers.

An early view of Ladram Bay, East Devon, showing the distinctive red sandstone pinnacle.

Budleigh Salterton beach, East Devon c.1910. Two courting couples sit overlooking the beach at Budleigh Salterton, much to the embarrassment of a passing lady who hides her face with an umbrella.

Opposite: Repairing nets on an east Devon beach, possibly Ladram Bay.

Exmouth beach is shown around 1910 with a family enjoying the sands. A little girl is making sandcastles whilst her brothers pose for the camera watched over by their parents.

Dawlish, South Devon. The seafront is seen from the cliffs and a number of wheeled changing huts are shown on the beach. Behind them stands a wooden building on stilts, possibly a café or other changing facility. Fishing nets are laid out across the beach. No traffic is to be seen and Mather's Royal Hotel is shown overlooking Dawlish Water. At this time the famous gardens are not in evidence.

The River Tamar. The Royal Albert bridge, built between 1857–9, is shown spanning the river from St Budeaux to Saltash. It is a combined suspension and arched bridge. The huge granite piers on the Cornwall side dominate the local houses. A small fishing boat is moored in the river and further up a large sailing vessel lies offshore.

NORTH DEVON

The fishing village of Clovelly, that straggles down the steep cliffs in North Devon, was initially the property of the Cary family. The main street is stepped and constructed with stone sets. The simple whitewashed cottages, overlap down the street, creating a charming scene which has attracted visitors for well over a century. The boarding establishment, shown left with its flagpole, offers 'Refreshments & Rooms'.

Mrs Tremlett takes the local form of transport – the donkey. These animals were used to take goods up the steep street from the harbour, and were to become a favourite tourist attraction.

Looking up the main street. A small wagon stands at the top of the hill.

Steps lead up to a fisherman's cottage.

Situated next to the quay is a stone built lime kiln where the raw material would be brought by sea for burning. The end product – fertiliser – was then used on the land.

Local fishermen and donkeys rest on the pebbled beach. To the right is seen Crazy Kate's Cottage, said to be the oldest cottage in Clovelly. Kate Lyall saw her husband drown at sea from the cottage and became unbalanced for the rest of her life. The cottage still bears her name.

The cliffside village of Clovelly, seen from the beach. Large stones have been piled in the harbour and are said to have been used as ballast by vessels using the harbour.

The ancient stone pier was first built in 1587 by the lord of the manor, George Cary. Its construction led to the improvement and prominence of the village.

A fishing boat on the beach.

An old cottage in Clovelly.

The famous view from Hobby Drive.

All Saints church has evidence of Norman work but with later additions and alterations. The church is found half a mile from the village.

Lazy days on the beach with the donkeys at Clovelly.

The traditional North Devon port of Appledore is noted for its history of shipbuilding and also for fishing. The local fishing fleet is seen moored off the quay. At the bottom of the ramp a man with a straw hat and bicylcle talks with two local boys.

The River Lyn at Lynmouth, North Devon. The River Lyn enters the sea after flowing past the stone built, Rhenish Tower which was constructed around 1860 to store saltwater for indoor baths. The tower, a noted landmark, was rebuilt after the flood damage of 1951.

The lifeboat was pulled to the sea on a wheeled wooden wagon.

Opposite: During a visit to Lynmouth Alan Tremlett recorded the launch of the lifeboat. It was firstly hauled up the street by villagers.

Local folk watch as the lifeboat crew board the vessel.

The crew row out to sea.

Lynmouth is seen from the Rhenish Tower showing the famous Mars Hill with its row of early Victorian cottages stretching up the steep incline. At the bottom is the Rising Sun Inn and the whole setting looks far more tranquil than today.

This photograph of Mars Hill, Lynmouth, shows Seabreeze Cottage that advertises 'Apartments & Cloakroom'. Behind the Rising Sun Inn vegetable plots are seen laid out in rows on the steep hillside.

The Foreland at Lynmouth is shown with two vessels moored at the entrance to the harbour.

Mars Hill. This charming scene of old cottages is near the top of the hill overlooking the harbour and Rhenish Tower.

The harbour at Lynmouth is shown with the tide out and a vessel moored beside the quay. Although shown as a trickling river in this scene the Lyn became a raging torrent causing massive destruction in the early 1950s.

Lynmouth village evolved along the steep sided valley through which the River Lyn flows. This was to be its downfall in 1951 when an unprecedented flood swept down the valley destroying many buildings in its path.

The River Lyn flowing through the middle of the village of Lynmouth.

The landscape of North Devon was to have a particular appeal for Victorians and was often referred to as 'Little Switzerland'. The small fishing vilages became highly desirable havens for the wealthy resulting in the building of numerous villas across the coastline. The traditional way of life was to change as tourism became an easier way to earn a living than farming or fishing.

The appeal of Lynmouth and Lynton was to be heightened after the introduction of the railway in 1898. The tiny train is seen with a goods wagon and carriages at the station being overlooked by the uniformed stationmaster.

The charms of the village were soon recognised as a tourist attraction and paddle steamers plied frequently from South Wales. The route from Lynmouth to Lynton proved to be difficult due to its steepness. The idea for a cliff railway was instigated and resulted in a water-driven funicular railway operating between both sites. It greatly added to visitors convenience after it was opened in April 1890 around which time this photograph was taken. Each car carried 40 passengers but could also be used for freight. The cars took on 700 gallons of water to operate and the track extended for 862 feet up the cliff face. It still operates today.

Traditionally the coastline of North Devon was isolated with only small scattered fishing villages. The rivers that flowed down to the sea were a vital resource. In the quiet Lyn valley the water bailiff's cottage is shown with a rustic bridge crossing the river. Note the rough wooden structure standing against the cottage wall, covered with turf.

One the loveliest settings in the county is at Watersmeet in the Lyn valley, where East Lyn and Barle rivers meet. The cascading waters have long been a beauty spot attracting large numbers of people. Now owned by the National Trust the area's appeal has not diminished.

A short distance from Lynmouth, on the East Lyn river, is the small hamlet of Rockford with its inn. It is unusual to have records of such isolated dwellings and such photographs are of historic importance.

Another view of the hamlet of Rockford.

A traditional cottage, partly roofed with corrugated iron, overlooks the river and a line of washing is drying in the fresh air. The use of corrugated iron has saved many of our ancient rural buildings from deterioration.

A classic cottage with young onlookers is pictured at Barbrook Mill, on the West Lyn above Lynton.

At the border with Somerset a number of cottages are photographed at Countisbury.

At Brendon, above the East Lyn river, a boy stands with a horse and cart.

ON AND AROUND DARTMOOR

The deeply wooded Teign Valley near Drewsteignton is one of Devon's loveliest areas. The ancient stone packhorse bridge, under which the River Teign flows, is a popular local beauty spot.

Fingle bridge, a three-arched stone bridge spanning the River Teign below Drewsteignton.

Mrs Tremlett walks beside the East Dart at Dartmeet.

The famous clapper bridge made from giant stone slabs, at Postbridge.

The River Teign is seen at a low level in the summer at Dunsford bridge. A stone weir is visible under the central arch.

For the Dartmoor explorer the Three Crowns hotel in Chagford has been a favourite venue. The two ashlar-built granite houses were originally the town house of the Whiddon family. The sixteenth-century porch is a significant feature. Ice creams and teas are advertised.

A classic thatched Devon house with porch in Chagford.

The Dartmoor town of Moretonhampstead is known for its ancient almshouses, built in 1637. The two storeyed building with an open arcaded front (loggia), with eleven primitive arches, is thatched and built from granite. A date-stone is built into the façade.

A detailed photograph of the almshouses, Moretonhampstead. Mrs Tremlett is shown talking with local residents.

Children at play in the centre of Lustleigh, adjacent to its ancient thatched cottages. The leat is shown on the right.

Opposite: One of the finest period houses in Devon is seen at Wreyland, Lustleigh.

The porch of Wreyland, with a local resident.

Bellaford farm (Bellever) is a classic example of an early Dartmoor longhouse.

A thatched Dartmoor farmhouse with farmer's wife and children.

Feeding the chickens at Shilston Farm, Chagford. The central arched granite doorway is decorated with two carved quatrefoil designs.

Mrs Tremlett with a friend walks at Buckland in the Moor.

The driving of sheep across Dartmoor is a centuries old occupation. It is now a rare sight. The shepherd wearing a bowler hat is followed by a pony and trap. Photographed in the Lydford area.

These sheep have been marked with initials WEH and N. Photographed in the Lydford area and possibly showing Widgery Cross in the background.

The River Lyd provides water for a thirsty horse watched by a lady and girl.

Abbey bridge, that crosses the River Tavy in Tavistock, was built in 1763 and takes its name from the adjacent abbey site.

Tavistock Abbey.

The site of Okehampton castle is seen here covered with trees above the West Okement river. Originating in the eleventh century it was rebuilt in the 1300s by Hugh Courtenay, Earl of Devon, with numerous additions. The photograph was taken in late summer as evidenced by the corn stooks shown in a nearby field.

Mrs Tremlett in an unidentified moorland village.

Posting a letter on Dartmoor, location unknown.

An unknown Devon farm, possibly on the edge of the moor, acts also as a Post Office. Mrs Tremlett talks with the farmer over his half stable door. A sign in the small window, seen left, states 'Post office letter box'.

Close up of the farm door and post box.

Old cottages with hand pump and stone trough (possibly at Water, near Manaton).

Mary Tavy was once associated with copper mining. At the end of the village the mine Wheal Friendship was linked to Tavistock and Morwellham by the canal that was opened in 1803. The granite church of St Mary is seen surrounded by cottages that at one time were used by miners.

The River Lyd showing Lydford Viaduct.

AROUND DEVON

The River Exe freezes at Countess Wear bridge.

The old mill at Sidford.

The famous Butterwalk at Totnes is a series of merchants' houses that extend over the pavement, supported by columns. Some of the buildings date from the sixteenth century and contain examples of the earliest plasterwork in the county. Foot, the druggist is shown at No.55, followed by Salter and then Reeves.

A young girl poses near Meldon Viaduct.

An early view of Meldon Viaduct near Okehampton with a steam train pulling carriages. The viaduct was built in 1874 for the L&SWR. The 540-feet long viaduct is supported by a number of lattice piers 120 feet high.

A delightful rural scene of a horse and cart on the bridge at Stoke Canon in the Exe Valley.

Making hay on the fringes of Dartmoor.

Tossing hay.

Haymaking.

Loading up the harvest.

An unknown blacksmith forge, possibly in East Devon. Two posters advertise the Regal cinema showing 'Honours East' and the Grand cinema showing 'Escapade'.

Unknown Devon village.

Berry Pomeroy Castle dates from Norman times but the romantic ruins date from the mid 1500s to late 1600s. The gate-house is shown c.1890 covered with ivy, as is the front of the hall seen beyond. For a long period of time the castle was neglected and became overgrown. It is now restored and open as a popular tourist attraction.

Detail of Berry Pomeroy Castle gatehouse. It is shown before restoration, with Mrs Tremlett in the grounds.

A later view of the castle after restoration and vegetation cleared. The figure may be Alan Tremlett, standing in the doorway.

FURTHER AFIELD

A number of the slides in the Tremlett Collection were taken on visits outside their native county of Devon. A selection of these images are included here, not only to indicate the variety of locations but to further illustrate the quality of their photography.

NORTH SOMERSET

The market place at Dunster is famous for the eight-sided yarn market building.

Slate-fronted three-storeyed houses in a side street at Dunster. A small shop displays a poster for the *Daily Press* while display cases also show photos of old Dunster.

A back street in the coastal village of Porlock shows a cottage with a display board for the local omnibus service.

A delightful group of thatched properties in Porlock includes the Ship Inn that is advertising 'post horse and carriages'.

The view overlooking Porlock Bay.

Old Somerset cottages at Selworthy showing the bread oven on the exterior. Mrs Tremlett sits on a table.

The Royal Oak inn, Winsford.

NORTH WALES

A rare view of a horse pulling a canopied vessel up the Llangollen canal watched by a group of children.

The Snowdon railway takes passengers to the highest point in England and Wales, the summit of Snowdon at 3560 feet. The inventive Victorians created the railway, operating under the aegis of the Snowdon Mountain Tramroad and Hotels Co Ltd. The title is shown on the carriages. Its first train ran on 6 April 1896 and concluded in the only passenger death ever recorded. The railway was closed for one year, reopening in 1897.

This fine record of the magnificent castle at Caernarvon, North Wales shows the tide out in the Menai Straits and vessels moored at the quay below. This coastal site facing Anglesey was first used by the Romans. The castle was built by Edward I between the thirteenth and fourteenth centuries and is one of the finest in Britain. This photograph was taken c.1890.

Pandy Mill near Dolgellau.

CORNWALL

Old house at Tintagel.

Bude.

Cottage at Mevagissey.

Pentewan.

Falmouth.

Gateway at Launceston.